DARREN WRICKS

10 Things Black Men Shold Know About Themselves

To my wife, my covenant partner who sharpens me.
To my daughters, my joy and my hope.
To my four sons, my strength and my legacy.
To my grandson, the next light in our line.
This book is for us,
because when Black men rise;
our families, sisters,
and our communities rise with us.

Contents

Preface

This book was born out of struggle, reflection, and faith. For years, I carried questions about who I was, where I came from, and where I was going. As a Black man, I've walked through pain, doubt, and brokenness—but I've also discovered healing, strength, and truth in God.

I wrote *10 Things Black Men Should Know About Themselves* because I've seen too many of us living without the knowledge of our true identity. Too many of us chasing validation from a world that doesn't understand us, instead of standing on the truth that was already placed inside us.

This isn't a book of clichés or quick motivation. It's a mirror and a map. A mirror—because you'll see yourself, the real you, in these pages. And a map—because you'll find direction on how to live differently, think differently, and walk with purpose.

To every Black man who feels unseen, unheard, or misunderstood, this book is for you. To every brother raising sons, every father carrying weight, every young man trying to figure out who he is—you are not alone.

My hope is that as you read these words, you'll feel both challenged and encouraged. Challenged to confront lies you may have believed. Encouraged to embrace the truth of who you are.

This book is part of my legacy, but it's also an invitation. Let's rise together.

Darren Wricks

Acknowledgments

First and foremost, I give glory and honor to God—the Author and Finisher of my faith. Without His grace, wisdom, and strength, this book would never have been possible.

To my children, you are my inspiration. You remind me daily why legacy matters and why truth must be passed on. Every page of this book carries a piece of my love for you and my desire to see you stand strong in your own identity.

To my wife, thank you for walking beside me through the highs and lows of this journey. Your presence has been both a challenge and a gift, shaping me in ways I could never have imagined.

To my godmother, who poured love, wisdom, and encouragement into my life—your prayers and support built a foundation that still carries me today.

To my brothers in the faith, who sharpen me, challenge me, and remind me that we rise stronger when we rise together—this work is as much yours as it is mine.

And finally, to all Black men: this book is written for you. For every son, brother, father, and leader navigating a world that doesn't always recognize your worth—know that you are seen, you are valued, and you are built with greatness inside you. May these words remind you of who you are and what you were created to become.

1

Understanding Your Origin

L et me talk to you for a minute.

Being a young Black man in today's world... it's no joke. It's like waking up every day on a tightrope — trying to balance what you feel, what you've been through, and who you're expected to be. But before you can even figure out what to do with your life, you gotta figure out who you are.

And that starts with this one truth:
　You gotta know where you come from.

I'm not just talking about names on a family tree or some school history lesson. I'm talking about knowing the real story — the fight, the faith, the fire — that's been passed down through your bloodline. The stuff they didn't teach us in school. The stuff that made you who you are long before you ever showed up.

When you know your origin, you walk different.
　You stop looking for approval from places that were never meant to hold

your value.

You carry yourself with quiet power.

You recognize your worth.

See, too many of us grew up without the full story. And I get it. Some of our fathers weren't there. Some of our families were fractured. But that doesn't mean your story has no root. You come from something strong. You come from survivors. Builders. Warriors. Men and women who didn't quit, even when everything in life told them they should.

"All Water has perfect memory and is forever trying to get back were it was"-Toni Morrison

That's you, man. You're not just floating through life.

You're trying to get back to something—something ancient, something true.

You're looking for the real you.

And the more you understand your past — the more you lean in and listen to the stories of your people — the more you realize you were never lost.

You were just waiting to remember.

Let me put it like this:

You ever seen The Lion King?

Yeah, that old Disney movie. It hits different when you watch it through grown-man eyes.

Simba was out there living like it was all good — hakuna matata, no worries — but deep down, he knew something was missing. It wasn't until he looked in the water and saw his father's face that he remembered:

I'm a king.

2

I've got a legacy.

I've got something to go back and fight for.

That's what I want for you.

I want you to see the reflection of greatness that's already in you.

Not because the world tells you who you are — but because you know it for yourself.

Self reflection

Reflecting on my journey, I realize that even though I knew my father, I still lacked a sense of true origin. As a Black man, I've grappled with the weight of a history marked by separation and struggle. Many of us find ourselves seeking solace and purpose in various avenues—some in cliques, others in sports, and many in religion.

For me, the path to finding my purpose led me to God. In Him, I discovered a source of strength and identity that transcends the limitations of earthly existence. The closer I draw to Him, the more I unravel layers of self-understanding, for He is the ultimate Creator, the architect of my being.

In God, I find solace in knowing that I am fearfully and wonderfully made, intricately woven together with purpose and intention. Through prayer, meditation, and reflection on His word, I unearth truths about myself that I never knew existed. His love illuminates the darkest corners of my soul, bringing clarity to my purpose and direction to my journey.

As I continue to walk this path of self-discovery, I find comfort in knowing that I am not alone. With God as my guide, I am empowered to embrace my heritage, confront my challenges, and fulfill my destiny with courage and conviction. In Him, I find my true origin, my true identity, and my true purpose.

2

Self-Examination

Let me talk to you again... real quiet this time.

See, growth doesn't happen by accident.

It starts when you stop looking outward and finally start looking in.

That's what self-examination is all about.

It's that moment where you slow down...

get still...

and get real honest about what's going on inside of you.

Not the version you show the world.

The real you.

The one you face when no one else is watching.

I had to learn that the hard way.

Growing up, I dealt with a lot — frustration, injustice, feeling like I had to always fight to be seen, fight to be heard. I was mad. And a lot of times, I acted out of that anger. Tried to control the world around me just to feel like I had some say in it. But truth is... it always landed me in the same place — stuck, confused, disappointed.

It wasn't until I came across this verse that something inside me shifted:

2 Corinthians 13:5 — "Examine yourselves to see whether you are in the faith; test yourselves."

That hit me like a brick.

God was saying, "Stop trying to fix the world, and start with the man in the mirror."

And I did. No
  I sat with that verse. I let it work on me.
  And I realized — I can't always control what happens around me.
  But I can take responsibility for what's happening in me.

That's what real self-examination is.
  It's not a one-time thing — it's a lifestyle.

Because the truth is: we change. Life hits.
  One minute you're strong and focused, and the next? You're drifting, slipping back into old patterns without even realizing it.

That's why you've gotta keep coming back to yourself.
  Keep checking in. Keep peeling back the layers.

And you do it with love, not shame.
  With honesty, not harshness.
  Because this ain't about being perfect — it's about staying aware.

7 Steps to Self-Examination
  Let this be your rhythm.

5

Pause and Reflect
Slow down. Be still.

Ask yourself: What's really going on in me right now?

Name Your Strengths
What's working?

Own your progress. Build on it.

Spot the Weaknesses
What keeps tripping you up?

Face it — no shame, just truth.

Set Real Goals
Keep it clear.

What do you want to change or grow in right now?

Take One Step
Start small.

One action today beats ten intentions tomorrow.

Check Your Movement
Are you growing?

What needs adjusting? What's working?

Keep Coming Back
This ain't one and done.

Keep checking in. Keep evolving.

Self-Reflection

I used to think everything outside of me had to shift first — the system, the people, the pressure.

But over time, I've learned... I'm the one who has to shift first.

6

Self-examination didn't just help me grow — it saved me.

Now, it's a rhythm I come back to again and again.
  Not because I've got it all figured out, but because I refuse to drift.
  And when I do? This process pulls me back.

So I encourage you: let this be more than words on a page.
  Let this become your rhythm too.
  A way of staying rooted. A way of remembering who you are.
  Because the truth is — you can't change what you're not willing to face.

3

Recognizing Your Value

"**F**ocusing your life solely on making a buck shows a certain poverty of ambition. It's asks too little of yourself. Because it's only when you hitch your wagon to something larger than yourself that you realize your true potential" - Barrack Obama

In this world, it's way too easy for a young Black man to feel like he doesn't matter.

Too many of us grow up surrounded by messages that tell us we're a threat... or a problem... or just invisible. And after a while, if you're not careful, you start to believe it.

But let me remind you:
  Your value was never up for debate.

It's not something you earn. It's something you carry — from the moment you take your first breath.

Recognizing your value starts with knowing that your voice matters.
  Your presence matters.
  Your story matters.

As a young Black man, you bring more to the table than people can even begin to imagine. Culture, insight, creativity, resilience — all shaped by what you've lived through and how you see the world. You don't have to shrink to fit into someone else's idea of who you should be.

Stand tall in who you are.

Yes — it takes courage to keep showing up in spaces that weren't built for you.
  It takes strength to keep going when it feels like the system is stacked against you.
  But every step forward you take is proof of your power.

Part of recognizing your value is refusing to accept the lies they've fed us — that we're only valuable if we fit into a box. Or stay quiet. Or play the role.
  Nah. That's not us.

We're not problems to be fixed — we're purpose walking.

But too many times, we chase success thinking it'll prove our worth.
  That's why some of us hustle the streets. That's why we chase fast money, get caught up selling drugs, or grind ourselves down chasing a dollar.
  But that kind of success without purpose? It never satisfies.

We were never meant to chase success.
  We were built to chase purpose — and let success find us as a result.
  Because when you know your value, you stop trying to be seen and start living with vision.

And here's something else:
  Your value isn't just in what you do. It's in what you've been through.

The pain, the pressure, the process — all of it matters.

9

But only if you capture it.

Start writing things down.
    Record the moments.
    Track the growth.
    Because what you've lived through? That's gold. That's your value.
    And one day, those same moments could be the exact thing that opens a door, heals somebody else, or builds the legacy you were born to leave.

You are the value.
    Don't let anybody make you forget that.

And don't just recognize it for yourself — advocate for your brothers too.
    Speak up when things aren't right.
    Fight for what's fair.
    Stand in the gap when somebody else forgets who they are.

Because when you really know your value, it's not just about you anymore — it becomes about lifting up your people too.

Self-Reflection

As a young Black man, you've got to embrace your struggle, your hustle, and your story.
    That's what sets you apart. That's what makes you real.

Don't let anybody tell you otherwise.

You've been through the fire.
    You've faced the hate.
    And still — you rise.

That's the spirit of a warrior.

That's the heart of a king.
Own that. Embrace that. Let it fuel your fire.

But don't stop there. Recognizing your value means standing up.
Not just for yourself, but for your brothers.
It means demanding respect. Demanding justice.
Demanding what's rightfully yours.

In a world that tries to cage us, strip us of our dignity and worth —
you've got to fight to remember who you are.

Let's be real — the jail system wasn't built to reform us.
It was built to break us.
To strip us of our humanity. To reduce us to a number.

They lock us in cages like we ain't worth nothing.
But they can't touch what's inside of us.
They can't chain our minds.
They can't silence our dreams.
They can't erase the kings we are at our core.

Too many of us have been caught in their web —
swallowed by the belly of the beast.
But somehow, we still rise.
We rise because we know our worth.
Because we refuse to be defined by their labels and lies.

So hold onto your worth like it's your most precious possession —
because it is.

No matter what they throw at us,
we keep rising.

That's the power of knowing your value.

That's the power of being a Black man in America who refuses to forget who he is.

So my brothers —

Never forget your worth.

You are more than just a statistic.

More than just a stereotype.

You are a force.

A voice.

A light.

A king in your own right.

Walk like it.

Speak like it.

Live like it.

And never let anybody dim your shine.

4

Navigating Motivation

L et's talk about it—motivation. That fire in your chest. That push in your gut. That whisper that says, "Keep going, even when it hurts." See, motivation is like gas in the tank. Without it, you're stuck. But let's be real—it don't always come easy, especially when life got hands and you feel like you catchin' every single one.

I done had days where I didn't wanna get up. Days when the dream felt far. Days when the noise in my head was louder than the vision in my heart. But what I learned is this—motivation don't always show up on its own. Sometimes, you gotta go find it. Sometimes, you gotta build it from the ground up.

First thing you gotta do is figure out what fuels you. What gets you out the bed when your body say "nah"? What makes you push when your mind say "quit"? Is it your kids? Your mama? That dream you been sitting on since high school?

Whatever it is—lock in. Write it down. Keep it in front of you. 'Cause when the storm comes—and it will—you gon' need that reminder of why you started in the first place.

Here's the truth: motivation ain't always gonna tap you on the shoulder like, "Hey, let's grind today." Nah. Most times, it's quiet. You gotta go get it. That means setting real goals. Breaking 'em down. Taking baby steps if you have to. One page. One rep. One small win at a time.

Consistency is louder than motivation. Show up even when you don't feel like it—and watch that fire come back stronger.

Your spark might come from anywhere. Your brothers pushing you. Your kids watching you. Even your haters doubting you. Use it all. Let every challenge, every setback, every "you can't"—fuel you. Don't waste pain. Let it push you closer to your purpose.

Now here's where it gets real strategic—understand how you move. Some of us learn best by hearing it. Others gotta see it. Some of us don't learn nothin' unless we do it with our own two hands.

You a hands-on learner? Cool—get in the field. Mess up. Learn from the bruises. You more visual? Make that vision board, write affirmations, paint the picture till it's clear. More of a lone wolf? Cool. Find your rhythm, create that zone, and get in it. Knowing how you work will help you stay lit even when life try to blow the flame out.

Some of us thrive with a squad. That team energy, that group accountability— it keeps us locked in. Others? We like to move solo. That don't mean we ain't working—it just means we got our own pace, our own lane.

Figure out where you fit. And whether you ride with a crew or roll alone, make sure you stay focused and intentional. Don't just move—move with meaning.

Let's keep it 100—there'll be days when you ain't got it. Days when the flame's low, and all you feel is stuck. That don't mean you failed. That means you human.

That's when you gotta switch it up. Try something new. Reignite the spark. Revisit your "why." Take a break if you need to—but don't quit. The fire might flicker, but it ain't out. You still got it in you.

Self reflection

I had to learn this the hard way. From Mickey Mouse schools in the city to the silence of Racine's suburbs—I lost motivation more times than I can count. But every time I got close to giving up, I remembered why I was grinding in the first place. Not just for me—but for the ones coming behind me. For the younger me who never had a blueprint. For my sons.

Motivation ain't magic. It's a muscle. And the more you work it, the stronger it gets.

Reflection Questions

- What truly motivates you—and why?
- How do you respond when your motivation is low?
- What can you do this week to reignite your drive?

Bottom line: Don't wait on motivation to find you. Go chase it. Build it. And when it gets tough—remember you were built tougher.

5

Fatherhood: Embracing the Sacred Duty

"The strongest, toughest men all have compassion. They're not heartless and cold. You have to be man enough to have compassion - to care about people and about your children."

• Denzel Washington

Let's talk about something sacred-fatherhood.

One of the heaviest, most beautiful, most important callings we'll ever carry. And I ain't talking about

just making kids-I'm talking about raising them. Loving them. Covering them.

See, being a father ain't about being some superhero in a cape. It's about showing up. Over and

over again. Through the good, the rough, the messy, and the uncertain.

Be Present

The first and most powerful thing you can give your child is your presence...

Be Attentive

16

Don't just hear-listen. Pay attention to what lights them up...

Be Involved

Get in it. Not just from the sidelines-get in the game...

Be Honest About the Struggle

Now look-fatherhood ain't easy. There'll be days where you feel like you're messing it all up...

Be the Example

Your child is learning how to be a man, how to love, how to deal with pressure...

Be Love, All the Way Through

At the core of it all is love. Not the kind that fades when life gets hard, but the kind that holds on...

I ain't write this from theory-I wrote this from experience...

That's where the healing begins-Not just for them, But for you too.**Reflection Questions**

How present are you with your kids-not just physically, but emotionally?

What does your child need from you that you haven't been giving lately?

What legacy are you building, right now, in the way you father?

Reclaiming the Image of the Black Father

Now before we even go deeper, let's call out the lie that's been floatin' around for way too long...

Fatherhood Ain't About Perfection-it's About Presence

Being a father ain't about having all the answers. I'll be the first to say-I messed up...

In the Hood, Fatherhood Hits Different

When you're raisin' kids in the hood, everything gets magnified...

Changing the Narrative, One Life at a Time

We gotta push back against these stereotypes with our lives...

Lifting Each Other Up

This ain't a solo journey, either. We need to hold each other down...

Self reflection

I didn't always have the blueprint, but I had the desire. I had pain, but I also had purpose...

Reflection Questions

What kind of legacy do you want to leave as a father or future father?

How are you breaking or healing the generational patterns you were handed?

Who in your community can you support or mentor as a father figure?

Bottom line

We ain't just fathers-we're foundation layers. Let's keep building. Let's keep loving. Let's keep

showing the world what Black fatherhood really looks like.

6

Navigating Leadership

Listen—
   I learned something the hard way:
   There's a time to *follow*,
And there's a time to *lead*.
Knowing the difference?
That right there can shift your entire life—
Your growth, your relationships, your direction.
Let's be clear—
Following ain't weakness.
It don't mean you're soft.
And it sure don't mean you're letting somebody else run your life.
Sometimes, following is the most grounded,
Most humble, most *strategic* thing you can do.
I've learned from people who were ahead of me.
Older. Wiser.
Didn't have it all perfect—
But they had something I needed.
I watched how they moved.
I paid attention to how they carried themselves.
I picked up what they didn't even know they were teaching.
And my mom—

She didn't raise me in church,
But she raised me to observe.
She had a wisdom that came from experience,
Not from titles.
And when I felt that pull—
That sense that something bigger was calling me—
That's when I started walking.
Not because someone dragged me,
But because *God was drawing me.*
Even now, I'm still learning from the ones around me.
Even from my own son.
Because leadership don't mean you stop learning.
It means you stay open.

Following means you're teachable.
Willing to listen.
Willing to grow even when you're unsure.
That's leadership, too.
But eventually, you feel the *tug*—
"It's your turn now."
Maybe nobody else in your circle is stepping up.
Maybe people are watching how you move.
That's when you lead.
Not with ego—
But with *purpose.*
Not to flex—
But to *serve.*

Let me tell you something:
Leadership ain't about being the loudest.
It's having the courage to do what's right,
Even when it's hard.
It's knowing when to speak,

And when to stay quiet and *listen*.
It's making space for others to grow
While you keep growing, too.
Because real leaders never stop learning.

If you're part of a team—
Family.
Work.
Ministry.
Your circle—
Leadership doesn't mean taking over.
It means contributing.
Building.
Lifting people up instead of tearing them down.
Here's how that looks in real life:

Lead by Example
Show up.
Be consistent.
Let your actions speak—
People watch more than they listen.
Communicate Real
Be honest.
Be clear.
Don't just talk—*listen*.
That's how trust gets built.
Know Your Lane
Play to your strengths.
God gave you gifts—*use 'em*.
That's how teams win.
Build Others
This ain't a one-man show.
Share knowledge.

Offer help.
Push your people to shine.
Stay Flexible
Life don't move in straight lines.
Be willing to shift, adjust,
Grow with the team.
Build Trust
Learn your people.
Respect their story.
Relationships fuel results.
Celebrate the Wins
Big or small—acknowledge progress.
Gratitude is fuel.
Recognition is glue.

Look—
I've worn a lot of hats:
Soldier.
Father.
Friend.
Hustler.
Preacher.
And through it all, I've learned:
Whether I'm leading or following,
What matters most is staying *grounded*,
Staying *humble*,
And letting *God* guide my steps.

So wherever you are on your journey,
Just know this—
You don't gotta have it all figured out to start walking.
Just take the next step.
And if you fall?

Get up.
Follow when you need to.
Lead when you're called.
And *never forget who you are.*

You don't become a leader the day someone gives you a title.
You become a leader the moment you choose **responsibility over comfort.**

Leadership ain't a job description.
It's a mindset.
It's a *calling.*
And for Black men especially,
Leadership comes with a unique weight—
And a unique opportunity.
Too often, we're seen as threats
Before we're seen as leaders.
But that just means—
We gotta move *different.*
We gotta lead with *vision*, not just volume.

Whether you're leading in your home,
Your community,
At work,
Or inside yourself—
This chapter right here
Is about helping you do it with clarity, confidence, and conviction.

1. Leadership Starts Inside
Before you can lead anybody else,
You gotta lead yourself.
Your emotions.
Your habits.
Your decisions.

Self-discipline is the foundation.
Without it?
Everything crumbles.

2. You Don't Need Permission to Lead

Don't wait for a title, a degree,
Or approval from folks who don't know your story.
If you see a gap—*fill it.*
If you see a need—*meet it.*
Leadership is about *initiative*,
Not position.

3. Leadership Isn't Loud

You don't have to shout to be heard.
Some of the strongest leaders move in silence—
And let their fruit speak.
Control your presence.
Move with intention.
Let your *impact* echo.

4. Servanthood is Power

Leadership ain't about flexing.
It's about *serving.*
Washing feet.
Listening to pain.
Showing up when it's inconvenient.
Real power lives in humility.

5. Know the Weight You Carry

You represent more than yourself.
That's not fair—
But it's *real.*
Every room you enter,

Every board you step on,
Every table you sit at—
You're breaking something open
For the ones coming behind you.
Walk *aware*,
Not afraid.

6. Lead with Love, Not Ego

Ego says, "It's about me."
Love says, "It's about us."
Ego divides.
Love *unites*.
If you're not leading with love,
You're leading with something dangerous.

7. Leadership Requires Listening

Too many folks want to be heard—
But don't want to *hear*.
A wise leader listens twice as much as he talks.
Learn your people.
Understand their needs.
Meet them where they are.

8. Your Pain Has Purpose

Some of your strongest leadership moments
Will come out of your *darkest* seasons.
The loss.
The rejection.
The struggle.
Don't waste that pain.
Use it to guide others through *theirs*.

9. Build Bridges, Not Thrones

It ain't about ruling over people—
It's about building *with* them.
Empower others to lead too.
A real leader multiplies—
He don't hoard.

10. God is Your Guide

There'll be days when the weight feels too heavy.
That's when you lean on the One
Who called you to it.
Prayer.
Wisdom.
Grace.
Stay rooted in something bigger than yourself.
That's how you stay *steady* when the storms come.

Reflection Questions:

Where in your life are you being called to lead right now?
What's one area you need to strengthen to lead well?
Who are you leading—and are they better because of it?

Leadership ain't about perfection.
It's about **consistency**,
Character,
And **courage**.
And Black man—
You've got what it takes.

7

Practicing Prudence: Navigating Wise Choices

"The prudent see danger and take refuge, but the simple keep going and pay the penalty."Proverbs 27:12

Let's talk about prudence.

It's not a word you hear every day-But it's one of the most essential tools a man can walk with.

Prudence is wisdom in motion. It's the pause before the punch. It's the gut-check before the wrong

move. It's thinking about the impact before the impulse.

And for me-that didn't come from books. That came from life.

I grew up in Chicago. And no, I wasn't out here looking to prove I was hard. That wasn't me. But I

was tested. Picked on. Challenged.

And I didn't like fighting. But I did what I had to do to stand my ground.

Still-even in the heat of those moments, there was always something in me saying, "Don't move

yet." "Look at the bigger picture."

I didn't call it discernment or strategy back then. But it was there.

And when I finally read Proverbs 27:12-"The prudent see danger and take refuge..."-it gave

language to what God had already been forming in me.

Prudence is Power in Disguise

Prudence don't look flashy. It don't show off. It don't shout.

But it protects. It preserves. It positions you to win long-term.

People think real power is being quick to react-But the truth is, real power knows when to wait.

When to walk away. When to let the dust settle.

That's not fear. That's awareness. That's maturity.

Prudence on the Block

I grew up knowing I had to move different. I was the only boy in my family.

That meant something.I knew early on-One bad decision could take me out. Not just from opportunity, but from my family.

From my future.

So I paid attention. I watched people. I learned how to read character. And most times, if something

felt off, I moved solo.

Yeah, I had my moments. I did some things I'm not proud of-But I did them with caution. Not

because I was scared, but because I knew better.

I wasn't out here trying to prove anything. I was trying to survive smart.

There were times I said no to situations just because something in my spirit felt off.

I didn't always have a reason I could explain-But I trusted that stillness in me. That discernment.

That's prudence.

And it saved me-not from one dramatic moment, but from a life of unnecessary battles.

28

Prudence in Relationships

Prudence isn't just for survival-It's for stability. Especially in relationships.

Not everybody who looks good is good for your growth. Not every vibe is divine.

I had to learn the difference between attraction and assignment.

When I met my wife, it wasn't about hype. It was about peace. Clarity. Consistency.

Her energy didn't demand attention-it carried intention. That's what made me want to rise to that

level.

Prudence in love means choosing faithfulness. Protecting the covenant. Keeping God at the center.

Passing It On

Now as a father-I'm giving my sons what I never had: clear wisdom.

I tell them all the time, "You don't have to react. You can think. You can pray. You can walk away."

Prudence is how you stay free. Stay whole. Stay ready for what God is actually calling you to.

Practicing Prudence in Real Life

- Pause before reacting. Breathe. Count. Listen.
- Ask the cost. "What will this cost me? My name? My peace? My future?"- Learn from others. Don't wait until it's your pain to gain wisdom.

- Stay close to God. The Holy Spirit will guide you-if you're listening.

Final Word

You won't always get credit for prudence.

Some people will call you soft. Some will say you're scared.

Let them talk.

Because peace is better than pride. And your purpose is worth protecting.

brotha-Don't get caught chasing noise when God is building your future. Play chess, not checkers. Think long. Move smart. Move with God. That's how you win.

8

Understand the Spirit Man - Build Your Relationship with the Most High

"**B**ut the person who is joined to the Lord is one spirit with Him." - 1 Corinthians 6:17

Let me be real with you, young king.

We grow up thinking the strongest man is the one with the biggest fists, the loudest voice, the

hardest shell. But life will teach you-your real strength is in your spirit.

1. You Are More Than Flesh and Blood

Nobody told me this growing up. All I knew was survival. React, defend, grind. But I didn't know that

deep inside me-under the trauma, the anger, the confusion-there was a spirit man, a deeper self

created by the Most High, hungry to be seen, heard, and led.

I didn't meet him until I got broken enough to stop pretending I had it all together. After the Army.

After heartbreak. After hustling just to get by. I was tired of looking strong and feeling empty.

And that's when I began to hear the call of God-not from a preacher, not from a choir, but from

within. That quiet whisper saying: "You are more than this. Come back to

Me."

2. Spirit Man vs. Flesh Man

You got two sides warring inside you-the flesh and the spirit.

The flesh wants what feels good right now.

The spirit seeks what's good for you forever.

When you feed your flesh-chasing women, revenge, status-you'll stay hungry, always needing more.

But when you feed your spirit man-with prayer, with truth, with the Word of God-you begin to feel full,

grounded, and guided.

1 Corinthians 6:17 says, "The person who is joined to the Lord is one spirit with Him." That hit me

deep. That means I don't have to search for connection-I am already connected, if I choose to walk

in that truth.

3. Building the Relationship

Just like with any relationship, getting close to the Most High takes time, intentionality, and honesty.You don't need to come perfect-just come real.

Start simple:

- Talk to God like He's your Father, not some distant sky cop.

- Read the Word, even if it's just one verse a day.

- Spend quiet time, away from noise, to just sit and listen.

- Fast and pray-that's how you learn to hear the spirit clearer.

For me, it was in the still moments-early mornings before work, or late nights after the kids were

asleep-that I began to recognize God's voice. And it didn't sound like thunder. It sounded like peace.

4. Walking in the Spirit

Understanding your spirit man changes how you move. You start:

- Choosing peace over violence

- Speaking life instead of death

- Seeking purpose, not just pleasure

- Loving women with honor, not just hunger

- Showing your sons how to be soft-hearted but strong-souled

The Spirit Man is Your True Identity

This world will label you before you even speak-thug, statistic, threat. But the Most High already

gave you a name before you were born: Chosen. Son. Royal Priesthood. King. When you walk in your spirit, you walk in your real name.

Final Word

You can lift weights all day, make money, dress fly-but if your spirit man is starving, you'll always

feel empty. Don't just build your body. Build your spirit.

It's the spirit man that'll carry you when life gets heavy. It's your connection to the Most High that'll

give you peace when the storm hits.

Get to know Him. He already knows you.

How to Navigate the Storm – Finances, Emotions, Life, and Relationships

"**T**rust in the Lord with all your heart, and lean not on your own understanding; in all your ways acknowledge Him, and He will direct your paths." – Proverbs 3:5-6

Young king, life don't come with a manual, especially not for us. Most of what I learned, I had to learn the hard way—through scraped knees, broken hearts, overdraft fees, and long nights wondering if I was enough.

But let me save you some of that pain. Let's talk about **navigation**—how to move wisely through this life when you didn't get a map.

1. Navigating Finances – Don't Let Money Master You

I used to chase money like it was the answer to everything. Truth is, money is a **tool**, not a **god**. And if you don't master it, it will master you.

What I learned:

- **Budget** every dollar. If you don't tell your money where to go, it'll disappear.
- **Save** something—every check. Even if it's just $10. It's about the habit.
- **Credit matters.** They don't teach us this, but your credit is access. Learn

it. Guard it.

- **Invest in your future.** Education, trade, skill-building—whatever levels you up.
- **Tithe and give.** Not because God needs your money, but because generosity breaks the grip of greed.

"The borrower is slave to the lender." – *Proverbs* 22:7

Debt will keep you stuck. Discipline will set you free.

2. Navigating Emotions – Real Men Feel

We were taught to tough it out, not talk it out. But bottling emotions is like shaking a soda—eventually, you explode. Learning to handle my emotions saved my relationships, my kids, and honestly, my life.

What I practice:

- **Name what you feel.** You can't manage what you can't identify.
- **Talk to someone.** A mentor, therapist, pastor, or friend who listens.
- **Don't numb it.** Weed, sex, liquor—those are distractions, not solutions.
- **Pray through it.** God isn't afraid of your feelings. He gave them to you.

Emotional maturity is a superpower. It don't make you weak—it makes you wise.

3. Navigating Life – Play the Long Game

Life will test you. Setbacks, delays, detours—they're all part of the journey. The key is to keep moving with purpose, even when it hurts.

Lessons that helped me:

- **Make a plan, but stay flexible.** God's timing ain't always your timing.
- **Stay grounded.** Keep a circle that challenges and uplifts you.
- **Don't compare.** Your path is unique. Your race is your own.
- **Fail forward.** Mistakes don't mean stop—they mean learn and adjust.

"In all your ways acknowledge Him, and He will direct your paths." – Proverbs 3:6

Let God drive, and you won't crash trying to do it all on your own.

4. Navigating Relationships – Love with Wisdom

Whether it's your boys, your girl, your family, or your kids—relationships shape your world. Some are for a reason, some for a season, and a few for a lifetime.

What I know now:

- **Communicate with clarity.** Don't make people guess what you feel.
- **Set boundaries.** Love doesn't mean access without limits.
- **Don't chase people.** The right ones will match your energy.
- **Forgive.** Not for them—for you. Don't let bitterness poison your soul.
- **Lead with love.** Especially with your woman and your children. Love is action, not just talk.

Final Word:

You don't need to have it all figured out. But you do need a compass. That compass is **God's Word, your values**, and **the lessons from those who walked ahead of you**.

Life ain't about perfection—it's about **progress**. Keep growing. Keep learning. Keep showing up. Whether it's your bank account, your heart, your household, or your faith—**you can navigate it all, with God at the wheel**.

10

Legacy & Commitment – Leave More Than a Name

"**A good man leaves an inheritance to his children's children...**" – **Proverbs 13:22 (NKJV)**

Young king, we made it to the final chapter, but this is really just the beginning. If you've come this far with me, it means you're serious about growing—about breaking cycles, building something real, and becoming the man God created you to be.

So now we talk legacy.

Legacy isn't just about what people say when you die. It's about **what your life produces while you live**. It's about what you leave **in** your kids, your community, and this world.

1. Legacy Ain't About Fame – It's About Fruit

I used to think legacy was about being remembered. But real legacy is about **what lives on after you**—your values, your decisions, your love, your example.

It's in the way your sons treat women. The way your daughters know their worth. The way your name is spoken with pride, not pain.

It's not about stacking wealth just to say you did it—**it's about building something that blesses others**.

"A good man leaves an inheritance to his children's children..."

That's not just money—it's mindset, morals, and mission.

2. Commitment Is the Bridge

You can't leave a legacy without commitment.
That means:

- **Commitment to God** – even when your flesh says otherwise.
- **Commitment to your family** – being present, even when it's hard.
- **Commitment to growth** – even when it's uncomfortable.
- **Commitment to truth** – even when it costs you friends or applause.

The world tells us to quit when it's tough. Walk away when we feel disrespected. Ghost people when we don't get our way. But commitment? That's kingdom work. That's manhood.

3. Break the Chains, Build the Future

Some of us are first-generation cycle breakers. We didn't grow up with healthy examples of love, finances, or emotional safety. But that just means **we get to start something new**.

You're not just building for you—you're building for the ones coming behind you.

Your commitment now becomes their covering later.

4. Make God the Center

If you want your legacy to stand, make sure your foundation is Christ. Money fades. Looks fade. Fame fades. But what's built on God? **That lasts.**

When I finally gave my life fully to Him—not halfway, not Sunday-only—that's when I found purpose. I wasn't just living anymore—I was leading. Loving. Planting seeds that would outlive me.

Final Word:

Your name is more than letters. It's a legacy.
Your choices matter. Your presence matters.

You don't have to be perfect—just faithful.

And when you walk with the Most High, your life becomes a light for others.

So here's the challenge:

Live like someone is watching.

Love like someone is learning.

And leave behind more than memories—leave behind a movement.

Commit today. Build legacy tomorrow. Walk with God always.

About the Author

Darren Wricks is a passionate pastor, a father, a veteran, and a relentless voice for truth and transformation. Raised in Chicago and tested by the streets, Darren's journey is one of grit, grace, and God's guidance. He is the founder of Children of God Ministries and a facilitator of emotional growth, identity formation, and spiritual restoration. With a background in leadership, church planting, and DBT facilitation, Darren speaks directly to the heart of Black men, urging them to rise, heal, and walk boldly in their purpose. His words are both a mirror and a map—calling men to remember who they are, and to build a legacy that lasts. Through every chapter and every challenge, Darren reminds us: we are kings in the making, and the crown is already ours to claim.

You can connect with me on:

f https://www.facebook.com/share/17DBUAoQHt

www.ingramcontent.com/pod-product-compliance
Lightning Source LLC
Chambersburg PA
CBHW011218120626
46545CB00008B/3057